This pestered isle

This

pestered isle

by Mel Calman

Times Newspapers Limited

First published in volume form in 1973 by Times Newspapers Limited, Printing House Square, London EC4P 4DE

ISBN 0 7230 0111 1
Designed by Philip Thompson
Printed and bound in Great Britain by Hazell Watson & Viney Limited, Aylesbury, Buckinghamshire

To the memory of my sister, Lydia

Introduction

by Mel Calman

THESE CARTOONS are a selection from those that originally appeared on the front page of the *Sunday Times*. The first cartoon in the book is the first one I did for that space—on 26 October 1969. The rest are in more or less chronological order—covering a period of three and a half years. When I went through the files, I was surprised (and saddened) to see how little the world's problems had changed during that time. Strikes, Ireland, Inflation, Unemployment, Bombings—all still with us. It would be foolish to hope that cartoons can change anything: all they can do is to make it a little more bearable.

I would like to thank Harold Evans, Editor of the *Sunday Times*, for providing the title of this book and for his murmurs of encouragement (and even smiles) from time to time. Also Duncan Gardiner, who shepherded my first efforts in to the Editor and softened the rejection of unfunny ideas with unfailing gentleness and tact. If there is any work worse than being a cartoonist, it must be having to cope with them and their temperaments. A special medal to Karen for bravery in the face of heavy bad temper on Saturday mornings. And thanks to Him up there for providing me with so much material to work on.

London 1973

Perhaps the new 10/- piece looks like the 2/- one because that's what it's worth...

Some people think
Father Christmas
is an illegal
immigrant...

I promise to hear no starvation..
See no starvation
Speak no starvation..
PRESS

I've a good mind to get inflation and then they'll be sorry...

This may be slower than the Jumbo - but there's a lot more privacy

I thought I'd buy one of those unbuilt houses with the wage increase I haven't had...

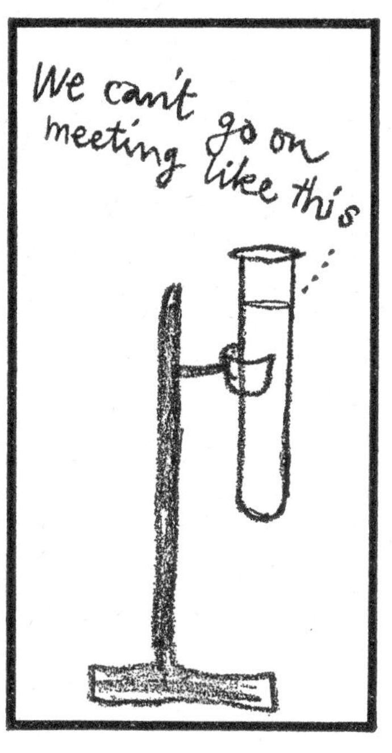
We can't go on
meeting like this

DOWN WITH EVERYBODY!
I feel that most protests only attack the fringe of the problem

Which should I save first - the sixpence, the Third Programme, the countryside or my sanity?

My nephew is at University - he's reading Files...

Voting's easy—
all you have to do
is put a kiss
against the nice man's
name

Let him who would cast the first stone - please put it back where he found it.

A plague on both your parties!
VOTE FOR BLUE!
VOTE FOR RED!

I'm not prejudiced -
but would you want
your daughter to marry
a South African rugger
... player?

I'm so old
I can
remember
Socialism

I hear they've brought
out a new pill that
stops you worrying about
the other Pill...

it's alright-
I'm only practising..
WALL ST.

FASCIST!!!
RACIALIST!
CAPITALIST!!
SOCIALIST!!!
Escapist

I've heard about these short cuts before

TO PEACE VIA CAMBODIA

I miss not being able to blame Wilson anymore for everything...

Wasn't the score once love all?
FINALS
Protestants
v
Catholics

Silence is more golden than ever
POST DEARER

I feel very nervy today

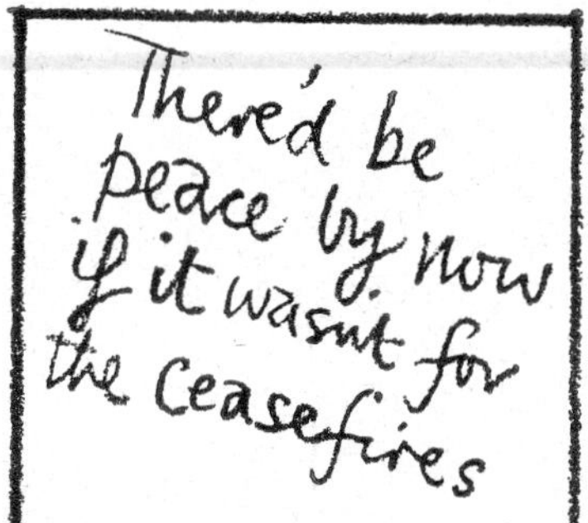

There'd be peace by now if it wasn't for the ceasefires

Middle East Conflict

Of course, these antiques are increasing in value all the time

BRITISH RAIL TEA DEARER

On a clear day you can see a better tomorrow ...

RISING PRICES
HEALTH CHARGES
STRIKES
DEARER FOOD
ARMS FOR S. AFRICA

I wish they'd stop shuffling the pack and get on with the game

GOVT. MOVES

Look at the exquisite drawing of the figure..
£2,300,000

If the lights were on, I might be able to see their point of view..

Sometimes I just
don't know where the
next 42 millions is
going to come from

RR

If I don't get better times, I'm going on strike

I wish I understood
·5 of this
Decimal made EASY
½P
?
HOW

Someone, Somewhere is waiting to hear from you

If we can now phone Shanghai – we should soon be able to get through to Holborn again

OUT OF ORDER

TORIES
WARNING!
THIS HABIT
MAY CAUSE
SOME
UNEMPLOYMENT
SoSMOOTH

I always did distrust these cut-price policies
TORY POLICY
We
cheaper prices

He then used a word that is no longer obscene...

A is for Abortion,
B is for Breasts,
C is for Contraceptives
ABC BOOK
E
S
X

I'm setting up my own committee of inquiry
FANNY HILL
DE SADE

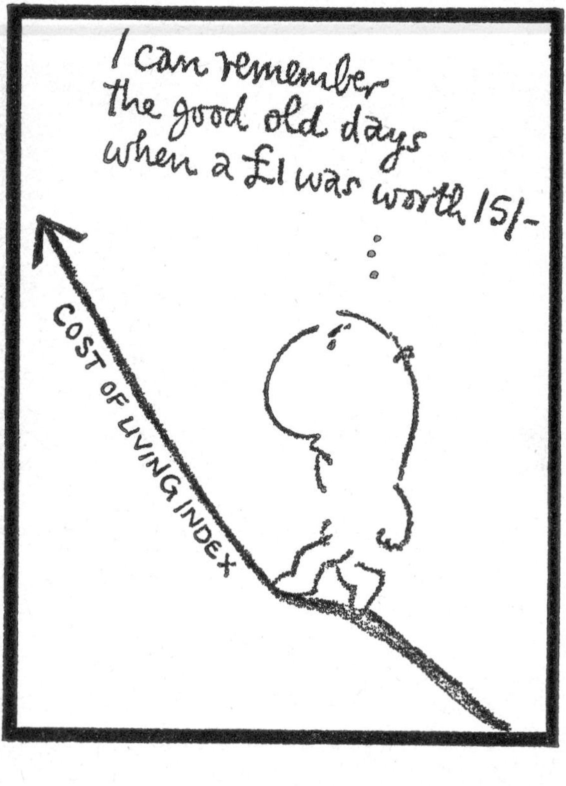

I can remember the good old days when a £1 was worth 15/-

COST OF LIVING INDEX

We're none of us
as good as we
used to be

Must be the only package tour not worrying about where they're going to sleep
MOON (LIVE)

shoot across

By Denis Herbstein and Derek Hum

[BRI]GADIER Marston Tickell, [Bri]tish Army Chief of Staff in [Nor]thern Ireland said yesterday [that] his troops would probably fire [bac]k across the Eire border if life [was] endangered by attack from the [Sou]th.

[T]his followed a 45-minute gun [bat]le between soldiers and [civi]lians near the border town of [Newr]y early yesterday morning. [The] border is now to be strength[ene]d with armoured vehicles from [the] Life Guards and the Royal [Hus]sars patrolling the South [Arm]agh area from today.

[M]eanwhile, the British Govern[men]t is expected to request the [Dub]lin Government to exercise [gre]ater control of the border, and [Bri]gadier Tickell confirmed that the [Arm]y is trying to establish its [posi]tion under international law. [So] far no shot has been fired at [gun]men fleeing back across the [bor]der to the South.

[T]he Northern Ireland Prime [Min]ister, Mr Brian Faulkner, has [bee]n asked by the Northern [Irel]and Labour Party to recall [Cou]nty and High Court Judges [fro]m holiday in view of the massive [buil]d-up of the law list.

[F]ighting broke out at the end of [a ci]vil rights meeting in London[der]ry yesterday. As the speakers [wer]e escorted by a crowd of about [...]0 back to the "free Derry" [area] of the Bogside, youths began [ston]ing a warehouse in which [troo]ps were resting and the soldiers [rep]lied with CS gas.

[Th]e stoning continued and troops backed up by Saracen armoured cars rushed at several hundred people who had come up behind the stone-throwers. The crowd turned and fled as the troops rushed at them.

Earlier Miss Bernadette Devlin, MP, told the meeting that the time had come to cease talking and to take action. "General Tuzo, Mr Heath and Lord Carrington have already started their side of the action by interning our men folk. They expect people to lie down and do nothing as they did in the 1950s. It is now a crime to stand outside your front door and rattle your dustbin to warn of the approach of troops. Now we will do the talking and we will do the sorting out of our political future," said Miss Devlin.

Other speakers referred to the

[T]HE ULSTER EXPLOSION: Pa[...]

I wish I could afford to be broke
EASIER OVERDRAFT

I'm ready to take his place at a moment's notice
LORD L. IS SHOCKED

DOWN
WITH
VIOLENCE
Anyone who tries
to take this away
from me
is going to get
clobbered

My wife
told me
to carry
this ...
EQUALITY
for
WOMEN!

I spy with
my little eye-
Someone spying me
with their
little eye..

SECRETS

I don't remember saying anything ...

Rho
rule

By Hugo Yo

MAJORITY rule in R be delayed for at lea according to the mo: tive statistical analysi able of the terms of th between Sir Alec D and Mr Ian Smith. most optimistic assum the pace of African advance—the vital qua the right to vote— suggests 2035 as the qualified Africans exceed the number c voters and be able tc from power. There Europeans and 5,200,0 in Rhodesia today.

The analysis, which done by Dr Claire Palle of Politics at Queen's Belfast, and an a authority on the Rhc stitution, appears in 16. It assumes absolut on the part of the Sn ment and its successor a major increase in th

esia: no Africa
or 64 years

ill
rs,
ta-
uil-
ont
ne
he
ut
al
or
sis
en
st
an
m
00
ns

en
or
y,
ed
n-
ge
th
n-
as
of

African schools, and full registration by all qualified Africans

On this basis, parity between Europeans and Africans cannot be expected before the year 2026. Nine more years would then elapse before school-leavers reached voting age and the electoral machinery for moving forward was brought into play. There would be swift progress between now and 1982, under the impact of the £50 million British aid programm the pace would then slow d

Problems of registering voters, of passing the fina well as the educational te of maintaining African un only some of the many im ables which in practice are to modify the optimistic tions which, in order to the complexities of predict Palley has made. But education alone, on a more mistic but still realistic assu —five per cent annual incr African education later century—the analysis shows century from now, in majority rule would still be years away.

Neither the British n Rhodesian Governments hav been drawn into publishin own assessments of this question about the settlemen would run a clear politic if they did so.

When I grow up I'm going to be unemployed...

Of course, there will be increased productivity - 100% more hand waving..
QUEENS PAY CLAIM

At least it's strike-proof...

I'm not redundant:
I've resigned:
1971
1972

it's not every
white elephant
that can fly..
...

This cyanide dump
set in an oil-slicked
sea ...

TRUCE

We've had it for years and still survived...
IRISH GET DIRECT RULE

It might be
a booby trap
HAPPY
EASTER

I think I'll just
mosey down to the
old shipyard..
TEXANS
RUN
U.C.S.

its another giant step for mankind and all systems go for the 7·55 to London Bridge...
N.U.R TO O.BEY

My feet would welcome another 'Cooling off' period

He who paddles
his own canoe
doesn't get
any bomb scares

What's democracy coming to when a man can't even go to jail when he wants to?

I prophesy that after due consultation and careful consideration of all the factors involved, fares will go up..

I hope it doesn't get wet and shrink even further
POUND FLOATS

Normal crises
will be resumed as
soon as possible..

Hurrah!
We've sold
the Concorde
to ourselves..

If they built the Concorde in Piccadilly, they could have two unnecessary projects for the price of one

It's a very shrewd attempt by the Govt. to revive the old wartime spirit

SHORTAGE OF FOOD!

QUEEN SAYS:

A dear day return please...
TICKETS
£5

Would you like
your daughter
to be caught by
a British trawlerman?

At least there's Lord Longford's Porn Report to look forward to...
AMIN SAYS
IRELAND
INFLATION

Now the smog's cleared,
you get a lovely view
of the cyanide dump..

I'm training for the
400 metres Walkout

INSIGHT on

The Munich Massacre

Four-page special, pp 15-18

its people like
General Amin
who give military rule
a bad name
UGANDA

I wish we hadn't all got our money on the result
HEATH to fight INFLATION

I was looking forward to
'The Slanging Match of
the Day'
NO
T.V. for
M.P.'s

Get well soon-
or I'll change you
into a yen

There will be a Freeze on several fronts, followed by a deep depression, and cries of 'It's all your fault!'
$
Adverse trade winds

MISS IRELAND

I saw three bombs go sailing by...
CAROLS

No-one wants it
FRAGILE
PEACE

its a full-time job trying to be an optimist these ... days

USA! 2 DEAD

SMITH & Identity cards

TRAIN STRIKE!

IRELAND

WOMAN BEATEN

And still got no sense
MAN 2½ MILLION YEARS OLD
NIXON WINS

Harold who?
HAROLD
IN
TROUBLE

What's the french
for – 'my postillion
has been struck
by a sack of
Jamaican sugar'

COMMON
MARKET
Phrase
Book

I'm not sure
I want to become a foregner...

WELCOME TO EUROPE!

He was charged
with being in possession
of an unlawful weapon -
a ballot box
EX P.M.
TODD
ARRESTED

I dont mind who knows about my bank balance as long as they don't tell me
CON=
CALLS
TO
BANKS

At least in the old days you could always put your head in the gas oven
STRIKES!
GAS OFF
FOOD UP
COLD PILLS

I think that's carrying nostalgia for the '40's a bit too far

GAS CUTS
NO TRAINS

BOMBS IN LONDON

Scale:
£
68p
Goodbye!
Pretend there's a worm-
I can't afford a real one..
N STRIKE
I hear Cunard is buying
a Concorde and
converting it into
a QE3..
Are you looking
for North Sea Gas?
No-I'm a
politician
who's out of
his depth
She's so dumb
She thinks
industrial action
means work..
STRIKE
NOW!
Inflate

or they'll all want some..
VAT AHEAD
There's nothing wrong with this country that a spot of wartime spirit couldn't cure..
BANG!
I thought we were at war..
BANK RATES UP
And profits..
LET THE TRAIN TAKE THE STRAIN
They've put VAT on Sirens..
I'm emigrating to the Scilly Isles..
GB

Just as I was perfecting my boiled egg flambé
GAS MEN BACK

That'll teach them to—something or other..
DEFEATS FOR BOTH PARTIES

I never thought I'd live to see the day..
R.I.P.
UNKNOWN SOLDIER
Peace in Vietnam

Oh, to be in England,
now that April's here..
SPRING
DAFFS.
10P.
plus. VAT.

Waiter! There's a VAT in my Soup

What's a nice girl like me doing in a place like this?

Here's to Nixon–
The Last 10 Days..

All I've ever been offered is luncheon vouchers...
SCANDAL-
BRIBES,
SEX PARTIES
TAX-FREE
PAYMENTS

I feel I lead a very boring life – Thank God..
VICE RING
SEX SCANDAL

For what we are about to receive may we be truly able to afford it..

I expect it's due to the increased price of bread
SAUSAGES DEARER

Give us each day
our daily price increase

THE

THE FUTURE

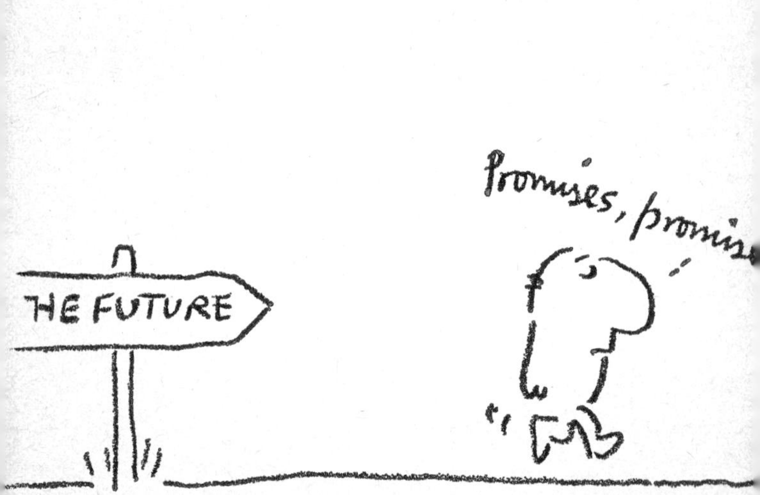

HE FUTURE
Promises, promise